Gross-Out Jokes

What do sharks call swimmers?

Dinner.

COMPILED BY PAM ROSENBERG • ILLUSTRATED BY BOB OSTROM

The
Child's
World®

Special thanks to Katie Cottrell for her
assistance in compiling source materials.

Published by The Child's World®
1980 Lookout Drive • Mankato, MN 56003-1705
800-599-READ • www.childsworld.com

Acknowledgments
The Child's World®: Mary Berendes, Publishing Director
The Design Lab: Design
Jody Jensen Shaffer: Editing

ISBN 9781623239961
LCCN 2013947275

Printed in the United States of America
Mankato, MN
November, 2014
PA02251

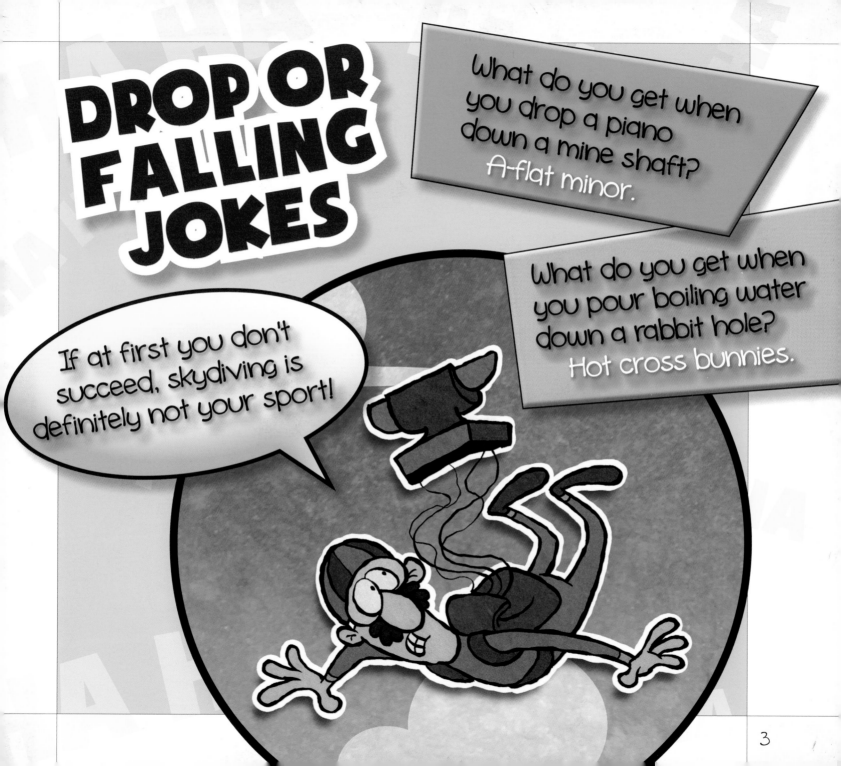

CANNIBAL JOKES

LITTLE CANNIBAL: I hate my teacher.
MOTHER CANNIBAL: Then just eat your salad, dear.

Two cannibals are eating a clown and one says, "Does this taste funny to you?"

Did you hear about the cannibal who was expelled from school? He was buttering up his teacher.

4

SKUNK JOKES

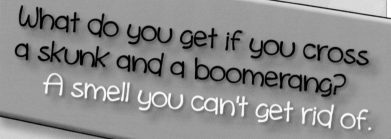

What do you get if you cross a skunk and a boomerang?
A smell you can't get rid of.

What did the judge say when the skunk walked into the courtroom?
Odor in the court!

What would you get if you crossed an alien, a skunk, and an owl?
An animal that stinks to high heaven and doesn't give a hoot.

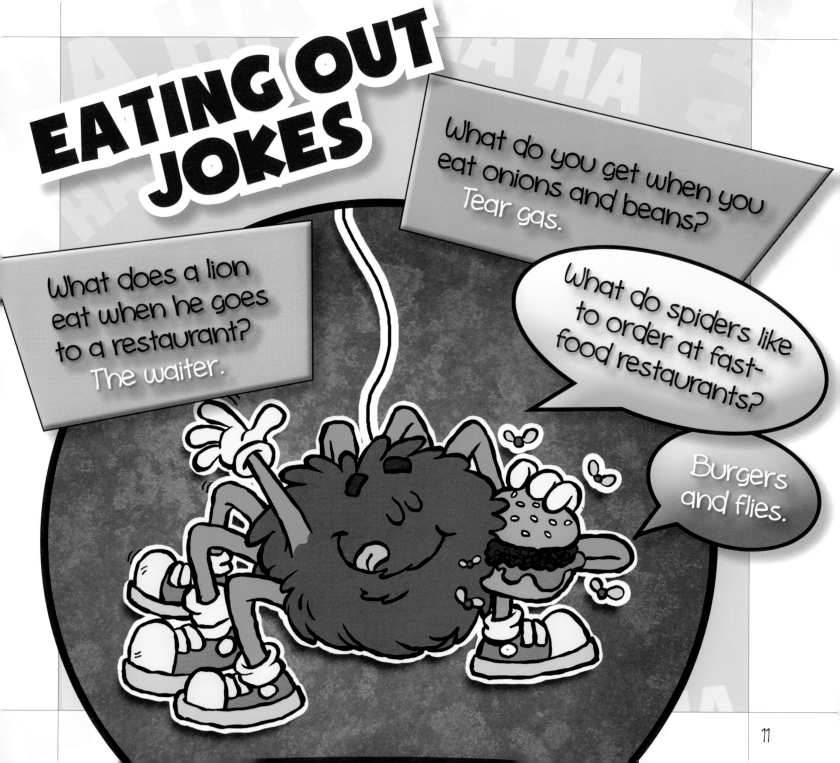

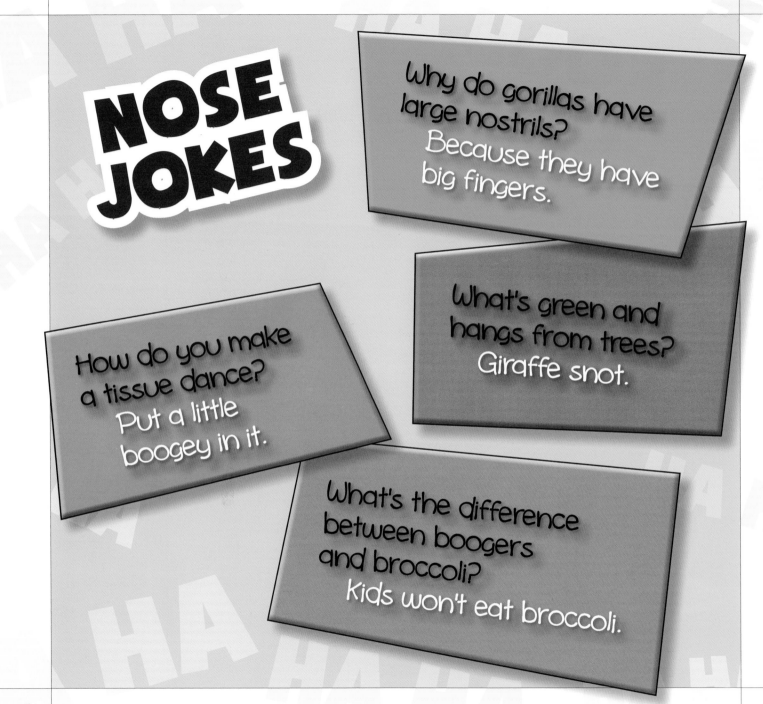

NOSE JOKES

Why do gorillas have large nostrils?
Because they have big fingers.

How do you make a tissue dance?
Put a little boogey in it.

What's green and hangs from trees?
Giraffe snot.

What's the difference between boogers and broccoli?
Kids won't eat broccoli.

BACKSIDE JOKES

What's brown and sounds like a bell?
Dung!

Why does Piglet smell so bad?
He always plays with Pooh.

What should you do if you're eaten by an elephant?
Run around and around until you're all pooped out.

What nationality are you when you're in the bathroom?
European.

What's the last thing that goes through a bug's mind as it hits the windshield?
Its rear end.

What do you get when you eat a prune pizza?
Pizzeria.

BOY MONSTER: Did you get the big red heart I sent you for Valentine's Day?
GIRL MONSTER: Yes, I did. Thank you.
BOY MONSTER: Is it still beating?

What do you call a man with no arms and no legs who's in the water?
Bob.

A man was working with an electric saw when he accidentally sawed off all 10 fingers. He quickly rushed to the emergency room. The doctor there said, "Give me the fingers, and I'll see what I can do." "But I don't have the fingers!" the man said. "What? You don't have the fingers?" said the doctor. "You should have brought them to me. We have all kinds of operations. We could have done microsurgery and put them back as good as new." "But Doc," the man said, "I couldn't pick them up!"

What did the butcher say when he backed into the meat grinder?
Looks like I'm getting a little behind in my work.

What do you get when you run over a parakeet with a lawn mower?
Shredded tweet.

About Bob Ostrom:

Bob Ostrom has been illustrating children's books for nearly twenty years. A graduate of the New England School of Art & Design at Suffolk University, Bob has worked for such companies as Disney, Nickelodeon, and Cartoon Network. He lives in North Carolina with his wife, Melissa, and three children, Will, Charlie, and Mae.

About Pam Rosenberg:

Pam Rosenberg is a former junior high school teacher and corporate trainer. She currently works as a author, editor, and the mother of Sarah and Jake. She took on this project as a service to all her fellow parents of young children. At least now their kids will have lots of jokes to choose from when looking for the one they will tell their parents over and over and over again!